[four paths]

Rose Hunter

*t*P
Texture Press
2012

[four paths]
copyright © 2012 Rose Hunter

cover artwork by Christine Hamm (skeletonjane.wordpress.com)
cover design by Arlene Ang

published in the United States by
Texture Press
1108 Westbrooke Terrace
Norman, OK 73072
phone: 405-314-7730
e-mail: texturepress@beyondutopia.com

for ordering information,
visit the Texture Press website at
www.texturepress.org.

ISBN-13: 978-0615715032
ISBN-10: 0615715036

BISAC: Poetry / Women Authors

Contents

iv
carricitos

i

la lancha

[path]

the path blazes through a tinderbox wedding cake
if it were carrot cake and who
                would do that   grey hair weeds and baths
grasshoppers i say seeing they are birds   locusts he
says seeing we are two
packhorse he says   carrot cake i say hmm i say laugh
two years long enough to be strangers but know this
he likes to see me suffer
our footsteps on the path   a trudge and a smudge if a smudge were
to rub a little of it out if i mention a lion
has read a book in which
the sun is a character
whereas those are termites
things like this he knows   definitively there will be nothing left of that
                                          tree

finding that impressive   arboreal even
like at home depot taking photographs while   his free arm forms a why
wheelbarrows and paint cans
are interesting if you are not interested
in that way purposeless in that way
kind   if we could be

the nature of this path   *hotter*
than the hinges of hell and i wonder
hotter than unimaginably
holding this furnace up
and if i yell it   makes sense between us although i
think he has taken none of my expressions
        in that way iron warping like
and in front turn trail behind us

[pampas grass]

do something even if it's wrong

people
betray how they feel when they say your name   an
over insistence or germ of some
monstrous growth yet   i liked how he said
               it seemed

like wine let's say burgundy let's say anything   but cherry
red with watermarks   a dirty
palette   dipping ready
this truck is cat like it's no surprise
jaw smash teeth crush headlight
clear through with the baseball
paint raked and hamburger ding dong
rhomboidal
mitsubishi   city skyline within
estacionamiento exclusivo
or   limp that's your job
signpost pencil grip
remember them from school
a yellow one got dirty like that too
fingers are like air in that they contain grime
               fingers are like parking lots in that they contain oils
a firecracker   is like sun on the corner of a windscreen
stomped by the wiper   a stroke of light
pampas grass   to work with it you need thick gloves   or
it will tear you with tiger's teeth   i know a lion would know
about pampas grass   although we have never talked about it
strikes me as similar to bamboo
in that it is thicket like but he does not like
ficus which strikes me as similar in that it is thicket like
he does not like ficus to the extent
you'd think he was talking about a person
who wronged him
and not just one of those he doesn't talk to
for a year the reasons   he does not like ficus are that it is
ugly and noxious   and quick to become
ugly and noxious quick
               i had never considered how ugly ficus was until he turned my eyes to it
then i saw it was filled with mud and decaying birds

10

and whereas i was never clean enough for him
i tried but it was an impossible task
and also i cannot think of a less feng shui plant can you
carnival grounds after the carnival
pruned to a feathered not plumage but cap
a stinky bouquet or that guy's mushroom hair that was awful
he's dead now so how bad is it main thing
i remember his hair   how he set it alight
to get a drink

fish bait c and trawling red
california and the number in blue   plates with no palms
like *please tell me what's* not *there*
please tell me the things that are not in it
                    i was devastated but after
hooked off   only thing i want
to live always somewhere with palms   or cactus
he called that doubling up but I thought not what else
can we say a few times
that we will then think is true   i won't know
but wish i'd brought up pampas grass before
it was too late now i will never know his feelings about pampas grass
but think maybe he likes it
he likes bamboo and pampas grass
strikes me as similar to bamboo
in that it is thicket like but he does not like
ficus which strikes me as similar in that it is thicket like

[taxi]

i want to understand you and i want to understand a path
like was that mesquite i forgot to ask
                and why that blue's so awful i didn't know
what this was going to come to and it was the first time i'd proceeded in that way
                in that way courageous in that way
regret
that i cannot re experience
that i did not experience why i'd try
                confusion was nothing like a thicket   and re the
                                                specifics
there never was a you   i should not look for one here
black spiders snapped elbow mangled alphabet   you miss
the north so do i   rockaway
if a lion thinks he's a turtle he might have a point for starters
he lives in a turtle house   and the bear i saw last in a teal sedan
with someone named lori outside the *surtidora*
he wouldn't show me his teeth
red glass between his knees
bear   sweat   he was still all me all mine
and i still loved it   partially
i knew it meant i was right to have carried the same
all those taxis around that circus city
and this lori taking him to pay bills
what i was doing then too
all that whizzing around with a bottle

[umbrellas]

i get the *elote* and he gets the *vaso* and to finish
leave them for the pigeon the skinny one
but the fat one flies up green and purple
hula glistening and here we have it he says
the fat get fatter and the skinnier get   i say
a lion eating corn anyway
can lead to a type of turn   for instance i know it's responsible
for the way he's looking at that girl   and how i'd like to
wear hardly anything like that   seem
hardly anything like that whereas my
little girl schtick   gentle heckler tagalong vibe
along for the ride   i'm too old for it
really   i think to be someone's appendage
                    pigeon's wing
if all i can do   is catch him in the flash
                    the perfect picture has everything i like about him stop
silver silver with blue trim
welcome to reality it's a painful ride
says big guru lion   *learn how to negotiate* but i say i will not
treat this as a stock deal and do not need to take advice
twenty nine years ago his last shot of dope
invalidated all i will ever say   i was ten
people look lonely when they're walking away alone
although you don't know if they are or not
and worse if they walk slow
i didn't know we were not in the middle actually then all i knew
was that under an unfolding
beach umbrella you were astonishing

13

[surfing]

this is all very much   taking up my attention and i wonder
                how afraid i am of things very quiet
it's always being delayed   that important conversation
in which we talk about
fireworks   or dreaming of the man who was stabbed and
believed you knew
to reach for me then whereas probably
it was a twitch or a tic   to watch what chutzpah
to head out into the waves   wind swell
not ground *if you quote me on that*
quote me right bo diddley jimmy page eddie van halen
covering my legs   my *lily white*
with mustard and cheese from famous
american hot dog she said maybe a *tejón*
cannot live like a lion exactly   but can let a lion live like a lion
live and let live   as he goes out
the way the waves and the going out into
the way the leash on ankle
the way the already decided the way   ain't nothing
gonna change between the way the now
and when he pushes the board climbs on paddles
green and white tumbling
pelican torpedoes and the frigate birds swooping in after
i need him to tell me these things like
if that would have been a good wave   why not
and *huanacaxtle* remember
they use it for furniture   the termites won't eat it
                the finer points
two hundred and forty emails
sixty of those his and one of them says he loves me
but which one and when he finds it there will be some loophole
outside the farmacia guadalajara *tacos de pastor*
i know my baggage and i ain't letting go of it for no one
i had forgotten he does not go *con todo*   and what
would a polished lion be
anyway   and speaking of
gemstones   *the distinction between*
precious and semiprecious
somewhat debunked   *but do not say*
i gave that to you say i facilitated you

14

in acquiring it
it was just an old curtain for my
doorway and rail with green paint
to clarify

but if he has to zig when i zag it's no big deal

[net]

but do not take me to a cabeza stand but
i had never eaten   *cabeza* that came later
except in *surtidos* and *carnitas* of course
from the fish tank   into the
how much can a little life
handle right now it thinks it wants a pink house on a hill
track down *garrafones* water gas   you were
a shock to first behold as it were
back in the room with the garden chairs again i
believed you did not exist anymore   that worked
but not long before you said
you want more   *i have more*
                    like the dead whale on your beach i
was not really there for the going
of the three legged bridge
in its place now this iron   cord like and
spinal eager to look   as though it fits in
the river sewerage pond monet lilies
horse heads bullets turned steaming rags
what can we do to people we can't shoot them well we can but we shouldn't
in front of the forty five degree washrooms bare feet
on the terra   and the monkey on his back decades ago
he put it on his foot and what he sees
new motor on that old panga and what about
our secrets like those cones   keep the net afloat
once he paid someone to listen to his   *con todo*
true this means   the worst thing he will toss out
but i know the worst is not the real worst
is something else inside that thing
the color of a cushion   dust trails on a curtain
                    full disclosure
to hide in plain sight   we know it
                    and no *we never talk about anything important*
you or i say   the net is green
you know not your green or a teal but an aquamarine

16

[eye]

and a lion does not know from
cheesecake   what i mean
to him it's just cheesecake   his symbols
inked on his skin whereas mine are way stations still i wonder
a ganesha on your belly is an elephant after all doesn't that
press on the solar plexus
diaphragm something   and what when you change your mind
that you haven't   astonishing
it was a series of coincidences and the odds were against
that chihuahua with one eye   and good
he does not share those secrets i've reconsidered
to stare at the black and the blue   his favorite colors
i liked them too must have   to keep those photographs
vapor trails and post
cyclone in the *lily white*
                    when you are looking out over what are you looking at
what is it like through that
to me those were frigate birds up there you say vultures
and that dog hanging off your back
maybe has some saint bernard
some labrador rottweiler retriever   and more
                    there's always more
guessing games for us

[sand]

and even as this girl
eyes dangling
                big gringo with money she thinks
like keys   i see him taking her home
his contempt for her would be like his for me
now or at eighteen   imagine it
it's only memory
                how he soothed my bear wounds
ten months ago this taco stand
waiting for them to fire up it was worth it
and the street dogs knew it
and when it comes to the sauce
he goes for the green he does not like to sweat when he eats
whereas i will heap on   the full catastrophe

              the man opposite he found him on the highway
where was he going he didn't know
but has been here since   this man and his girlfriend
have a child and a dog they do not wash
themselves their child or their dog i wonder
what it's like to be to be that sandy
and that okay   *something that's done but not finished*
           the replacement bridge
and although i would never say forever
to him quite rightly   sometimes a lie is nice
this sentence hurts around the sand area
the shelf the sea put there   that's right yes sir
with holes dug by beach creatures

hungry or full
a coffee a road trip and you
next morning singing   happy birthday
we love this story of how we met
who are you who cares let's go

[shell]

and was this when you were a troubled youth
thank you for putting it like that
but still i have no desire
to mow down street vendors
in this way a lion also has a shell
                    sometimes it gets thrown
asking me what my carrot is
there are no carrots it is not about carrots
you are not mine and i am not your
tuberous vegetable   celebrate he says
from a bear lair to a lion's den
is from xanadu to a turtle house
a better deal   there's food for starters
                    a turtle house eats cabbage and keeps on growing
but feng shui   even the dish rack under the counter
a turtle house is green but the cups are yellow and the bowls
and the cutlery has yellow handles
and there are so many banana trees
bananas in bunches what is a lion doing in a turtle house well
there's wall enough to bump and roar
but do not want people looking in   a bear obsession also
i can't get it who are   these lurking people
these peering lurking people
i would like to see in if to see in from in
were a talent i had
to see us in the light sitting   it's a
big turtle house more like galapagos
tortoise like   how they lug those rocks up the hill
and digging in the dirt   lion all over it loves
digging in the dirt   off his rocker i'd say
with lions parts chipping off   propeller and shrapnel and utterly
man   grinning *tejón* what
           gives   *tweaked*
about my daughter the rock wall   *and you* he says
ha lion all over it loves
this story   *man*   nose in the air *tejón* it's not
           funny
a rock wall can become so important
what happens when a lion zooms up to a meeting   late as usual
and burning rubber   he runs over a puppy's head

19

[turtle herding]

petrification permineralization and speaking   of bears
i am glad he was sighted   even by proxy
these animals she said
what are we to do
keep their coffee cups in our cupboards
not knowing that somewhere   they already took their last
                    i have a friend she is a turtle herder
she would stop the car if you were trying to cross
she would guide you across   read a turtle face
do you need rescuing or
the it's me it's mine   turtle responsible
i have no editing skills he says
but i say we say things before we realize what they mean
like a woman in a blue skirt
gets off at the town we don't know the name of
still i recognized her as redivider lady
although i didn't know how to talk about her yet   what objects to use
and was as he would say tenderized
                    when provoked i will say he can only configure emotion as pork chop
or marinating fillet   at a memorial
people go between their chairs and the food   coming and going i found
                                                                                        it
strange but why taking in death we are taking in
and the picture they passed around
in headband and biker jacket but he never rode a bike all i know is
they cut him out of two cars
                    a stack of white chairs next to a whiteboard
and when the page got to me they were asking
where is the page and i said here is the page
while trying to write on the page
what's important is to create the rest just is
                    i do not know the story you want me to tell
if it might be the one i want
but tell me no more of these sad stories
if you don't think they are sad
offer me instead fried plantains
or to drive me bananas tell me
i'm the only one ever called you on your rocky road
                    doesn't it contain marshmallows
doesn't count   i say if you keep them in a safe

anyone can fall in a pond or a lagoon   but can you fall into
a pelican torpedo is not certain it will get a fish
you are not a good negotiator   no quit
making fun quit laughing
                    if we go on a fact finding mission what facts will we
find   two wires and a light bulb do not
electrocute self no unless it's just like morning coffee
a bit of a jolt   *i know how to switch phases*
and your safe i glimpsed it   it was a defrosted fridge
and nothing in there but gemstones
whereas marshmallows are like buttons not hearts at all
the point is spend what you have and without consequence
                    come here come closer the bear he was more prose
in the way he walked and talked
and afterwards would put nothing away   whereas a lion is poetry
attaching to moments and objects and there is
nothing leisurely about you even when you are doing nothing
and if there's no bannister kiss maybe because
a turtle house   it doesn't have bannisters

[mega]

                    peanuts   to toss away the shells then
into the bank but couldn't because
you didn't have shoes you said i will buy flip flops and
i am doing that for you
that you can temper   astonishing   the flip flops
black or blue and marshmallows in the aisle
where you talked a woman out of living here
you and your *it's mexico baby*
the wild frontier   here in mega this woman
did not know her dreams were that silly   maybe
                    lion maybe   i would have objected but she was
hanging off you like hot *chicle*
and how you make fun   *a picture of this and a picture of*
i did not think maybe   i would never see this mega again but now i'm
                                                                                                glad
to have recorded an orange pelican and silver silver
that you are the lion who thinks he's a turtle
not the first case of mistaken identity for instance
i doubt you would recognize me as the *tejón* and i regret
i never saw that other *tejón*   opening your refrigerator
licking eggs   and sugar because *that's what they do*
lick things
                    look a mega's a big deal
on the way to a crane's hotel
end of the line in powder blue and crumbling   you share her history
the drugs they've got now
not even thought of then   to hear him talk
mesozoic   and true
we had to go past the dinosaurs
but the crane said she did not want peanuts because she just brushed her teeth

[teeth]

like memories do not belong to me
like shoelaces you can't tie what
i knew a lion could not become a bear then forgot
where are the sierra madres when
i accuse you of catchphrases and finally i said it
               clichés
shock a lion   don't give an owl's hoot
about clichés   or a turtle moan to get nostalgic
over snapshots of construction or garbage
at the marina take pictures of boulders
birds   mountains   huanacaxtle
where he couldn't walk   bare feet hot stones
said have a berry i said why   are they poisonous
berries are sad in the way teeth are sad
in the way new year's eve is sad there is
the feeling of trying too hard being overdressed waiting

[teeth] ii

like a turtle house glistening and facet marvelous
until talk of retaining walls   or boxing in that window
          look in all this if i want to know where is your home
it's more about you leaving again
the planning and the saying
along with the black and the blue
privacy is not mexican and the barking dogs
power outages and *laissez faire* waiters drive you to it
lions are not native to mexico and know
that day with the pronghorn i stepped through
          if a pronghorn asks you give away all your teeth
replacement bridge
redivider lady
sierra madres
because they are beautiful i said
and powerful and cannot be moved by me
          although a lion fits that description too

[fifteen letter house]

              hay cuartos   it says so
well sure   but what would you do
in higuera blanca   *you'd take pictures of dogs*
and horses   and we could get tacos i bet they're good
tacos are good even when not
         they are in this way like a path
empty
you are easily pleased and i was
pleased to be someone easily pleased or
to be so called in aquamarine
shoebox with cactus
mural   a western soundstage john wayne
can you believe it   while you
are wearing sunglasses and cowboy hat
you will never take them off
        again at all
what i mean is categorically   taking real estate pictures
it's easy to see i miss the point
all your pictures are low   *it's a dog's eye view*
sure but i told you   box in that window
i will find a room at the fifteen letter house
it was berry like crackling rotten   iron warp
i cannot proceed in order   you gave me a curtain
        stranger
and the *tejón* in your kitchen really   hearsay
i never saw her
the path is just a path the path is just
a path   it was nothing it was a dream it was everything

you were thirsty but i was busy
our thirsts will be quenched   i thought
soon enough but i cannot
go back for these photographs

ii

insurgentes

[room]

when a lion is not in the room with the garden chairs
he is all over the room with the garden chairs
a lion does not have one chair
a lion is not so like a *tejón* habitual
when it comes to chairs although it's possible
              he is more frequently to be found
on the right towards the front
that time i remember is nothing in its particulars
it's everything in its particulars
i was on the left   back corner
             for him and his asking   *and then*
to lead with that   perfect
for the lock and the key
but how does it fit with his feet so firmly on the terra
what you think matters to me no lion said that
was an ostrich kind of like
oppenheim's breakfast in fur
              ostrich out of water
crane with a puppy in her purse and a sea lion
talking about *it moved me*   what moves a lion
in this photograph leo line
yet will trust horoscopes what
when he is in this room and also
in thailand san francisco or minnesota
tearing around there is no end
to his vast carelessness
all the things   we didn't have in common
i knew to stay away from
my second most dangerous substance was
to stay away from this room
             between a rock a hard place and you
telling me about chucky who liked to hurt people
or your friend doing life once you visited it didn't go well
or your solitary cell with bible
and how you were   incorrigible

[kukulkán]

actually you were a mint sprig of
or an after dinner   this is not a lion shirt or a turtle
i do not know what this is really
that woman in green i saw her day before   and what's
with all the green   redux
thirty yards long and slithering
reflux and you
have friday and tuesday confused but no matter
                bright out and for once
i agreed we stood in dark glasses
is this one of those lies
you tell *for survival*   and who
was trying to kill you then lion
top of the food chain and you're not hungry
but of course the lie   to delve into it
the nature of what passed
between my excited really   and your

steamroller   amused   heartened
that you are not after all so smooth
                does a lion ever feel sheepish
unless the rough finish is the point
you know i will get it   eventually
and when i say know i mean
the anatomy of a lie   its aftermath and afterfact
one of those herky jerks
                and after all that's passed
re the shirt i tried to call it teal but couldn't
call bullshit call change the subject call
touch a baby foot
                and the way you do it like an auto part

while you shimmer minty and the woman in green did not
come along then with her popsicle actually
you told about a trip and i thought the long one
in my mind   kicking chairs
my fault i saw the cherry red
but went in anyway thinking i was beyond lion riling
turns out you are going on our trip
                lion all over

telling me about it while
a glove with six fingers
real estate bedspread green
if i feel like a fool
to have believed a shirt
for a minute   off the hook
i'd torch it although i tell a crane
i would rather buy a shirt than not
yet this one must have been
                         freshly ironed

and the woman in green i can't see her
ironing a shirt   why would i
and if i know a lion owns an iron
i know it must sit on the shelf
neglected
to be clear you seemed less lion like and i wondered
the woman in green   with the roommate who is an ironer
or the ex boyfriend who left an ironed shirt
you've asked her on our trip
like how it happened with us
plumed serpents not crocodiles and sandflies
but no matter you remember
who are you who cares let's go

                    not that you seem to know these plans
very well i already said that means you arrive
day after   stand in a park full of trash look
can't see a woman in green
gelling with your shrapnel and big guru lion
good luck woman in green or whoever is
not going on that trip   true we tell ourselves
stories to get away   for real
touch a baby foot
like a christmas decoration   with interest minimal or spring sale
outside the room with the garden chairs think look
what's an understanding between people   more than mint

everything should be harvested now but we cannot

[*columbina inca*]

i mean akimbo i mean under the sun
sierra madres and ornithologically speaking
no one is mistaking this inca
for a clay pot   or stippled roof top
light and dark and light   among the leaves
and blotty sun   i mean the dodge and burn i mean
          the whole bird
with not olive but ficus
bird of a scale its meaning and magnitude
i believed in that moment i knew moments
are not destroyed by their subsequence   monotypic
they say your disyllabic   call has you pegged as
no hope dove
          as gourd like you seem empty
as a three lights cry with that dark thing turning or waterfall
thunderstorm i didn't know what was leaving
only the smallness of what was left
i cannot be staunch
          as gourd like you seem full
as no hope is also plenty
          columbina inca i recognize you
as re divider lady
in grey parka and jeans lady inca
will have another slice of pie
and come in where it is warm

whereas bottle glass vial it was cold with you
whereas lion bear it was cold with you
memories of past warmth thin gruel
and other fabrications
          inca doves form pyramids
fluff out feathers squat down inca dove   sierra madre inca
already i felt i did not fear
black sand running what's left   in me
          i do not need to be staunch
jet eye slender beak wide pink feet
inca dove speak

[ostrich]

what an odd bird what a flightless shimmer
cancan dancer under misty arches
what a kicker while talking about mayhem
next to the taco stand   ostrich klatsch
makes it all personal or
ostrich in a grocery store
will read the fine print and if an ostrich
says he does not eat sugar   i do not believe it and say so
what i consider an unpromising start
discourse on the difference between artificial sweeteners that is
                    to get taxonomical   too quick and
to explain at length an ostrich will
psychoanalyze   sure
but anyone would seem an odd bird after a lion
reinforce it an ostrich is kind
i can dig that
                    and to bury his head in the sand
it's not even true but he will
lie low and press his neck to the ground
in an attempt to become less visible   ostrich futility
watering can on burning plain
with vase like curvature of neck
once i said i would treat a lion as a ming
take no lion to no fairs no circuses or and that he would do the same
it didn't turn out
so come here come closer adder neck
                    ostriches
wear pink as well as mint
but feel no need to call it salmon

[tongue feathers]

a rooster conversation with an ostrich
is of the type thinking a rooster could lay eggs
when what i mean is i think to leave now
would be a mistake   what he means
then again for reasons and how   a rooster conversation
has already shown me the concrete
and talk of saving it all year for christmas
i don't gel with that kind of long range
let's not have squabbling about the impossible
                    an ostrich wears the wrong kind of camouflage
and no monkeys on his back or his foot
but in his head   they talk to each other and what
monkey madness in an ostrich head
like if an ostrich thinks a *tejón* is a rabbit
tejón says she can hop to that
                    but an ostrich house in the night
locked from the inside this is not xanadu or a turtle house
nowhere to go leaving those
                    although you are free to do it   here an ambitious
hang out padded paws stained glass chopstick inmate like
an attractive prison although strewn with baby carriages
and the rooster opposite
shadow brick
                    with an ostrich you eat *cabeza*
labio and *lengua* and the lady she
picks out the cuts like those are a good pair of lips
lips are greasy like tongue is greasy
but he says depends what part of the tongue   and re the rooster
                    offer them two hundred
take it up the mountain
an ostrich whisking a rooster
is this what you call   hush money

[the lion and the ostrich]

there is always something else
that needs doing yet i feel empty
already like i never knew a lion not for nothing
we have a substance problem
sure   lion in my periphery and fidgeting
and talk of *forty clicks* it's like   sandpaper my eyeball
already   so why keep going to where he is
to make this irrevocable like the three legged bridge
                    washed away *and ain't coming back*
                    or how he *got dead and ain't coming back*
to *get dead* is like   what
in san francisco a bus and a bottle
next thing two weeks later   minnesota hotel
what i said   must have been glimpses
been telling that story so long he forgot
it wasn't a completely white wall
                    he's just a person with a hat
and probably not psychopathic
he gave me a curtain
it was nothing to him   not like *con todo* with an ostrich
it was immediately well we talked like you and i   never
went into the heart of   you know i tried to recognize
                    the independent existence of another person

easier said   i passed by that taco stand again
but not the same
i'm convinced we entered   a somewhere else place
where an ostrich could tell me about shoplifting and
                    for real red faced and wrinkled brow ostrich
whereas a lion is teflon seems like angles and ways to see an ostrich
and feel for the all and i cannot remember that with a lion maybe i should have
tried it or i was too often on the backpedal backfoot *tejón* tripping over
backwards i asked before what does it mean to fall into
something different a vat or a hat   macadamia or almond
right on   knee deep in the forepaw talk
lion not the way you leave but the way you are not here that's
                    glorious but do i mean you or do i mean everyone i get confused
helpless really   that look
next to the whiteboard that stunned
that jolt   that dropped veil and my hopes

35

                          i'm sure they're not right
and my dreams
                          i'm sure they're not right
a different path i thought re lion pain i had to smash it
but see where we are one week later
i know how to make the same mistake   in more than multiples
                     these are more than related skills
some people are about the petunias and some
about the addresses   i am about the petunias but then again
if i want the addresses do not
tell me about the petunias   this is what's called
a petunia conversation
if it keeps on i will leave   buy a map at oxxo
if a lion is with a serpent plumed or otherwise make sure
you are with an ostrich   same night
                     and told him if he continued   cancun was a trap
although i said i'd never been there
although some would argue i have
i'd say that was another girl   circus
minty   true
and if he sends me a postcard with or without a turtle
saying *be kind*   i'll torch it too
look   if an ostrich sees a mamey cart
he will chase it down   ostrich acceleration
and not to be exclusionary but no one
liked that fruit except us   not sweet enough they said
and we were the only ones knew what it was anyway
once i tried a mamey toss   that didn't turn out
although they are like little footballs
and peel off the bark mamey on my mouth
the roof it leaked that night
mango spritzer with an ostrich and he tells me a lion said
mo fo of a storm headed this way but we both agreed not so bad
what does a lion know anyway
up the alleyway and there were no toads
just three dogs and to ostrich past the gauntlet

just remember you're the guilty one
lion in the room with the garden chairs   only time i dared look at you
                     was when you leaned elbow on knee
and bowed your head top of your cowboy hat
tips of your ears and i imagined them
burning although they were not

[candy]

                        while this one with feathers said about candy
and candy eaters and i
said which am i and he said you're candy of course
and i said the kind with no sugar the nutrasweet kind
look last week was a long time ago   and what
i've learnt from bear experience
and what from a bird of a scale
an ostrich drives not like a lion of course
slow and hugging the side of the road
two toed foot riding the brakes ostrich caution and
firetruck red stopping at all the orange   in the rain sure
vallarta in september and to blur the edges
to drive south to the mouth is to pass a bear house
                    that *callejón* of course how much did i imagine
you with your red bottle

[jabón neutro]

deathtrap and loving it toothpaste tube i am wonder
seats missing and tunnel like
bam the pothole slam the brake
the button is where how to   stop this thing a rope
and those are baby sneakers   confirm
the driver may be twelve
hot as a mother and that window   don't open
tin can crack can makes me think how a bear used to
cut them open to get the last   is how i could
peel back this roof to reveal
                  the scene popping up
smells not of ash but soap   what happens
when this time instead of the usual
i am back   how it was
in the house with the talavera
                the yellow and the blue
gallery warehouse dining room table   veer to the right
other side of the hall   when i reach the other
side of the hall   and the pool the golf course
the son's birthday cake   like a whole city such a cake
flags and castles and petting zoo seriously
the coffee maker   i can't figure it this is beggars
being choosers beggar
with split head
              and the smell of neutral soap
now in the landlocked   villa of the sea
crack palace   took a sea lion to tell me that
astonishing   and then just information
            i do not need to tug that rope
to fall out past the construction
opposite the shoe store and next to the juice shop
how much did i imagine   walking to a bear park
calm past the river to you
to have a drink with you   *jacarandas*
lit up and i will see your teeth
at the bar on the chair next and if not then   later
            you will show me your teeth

[natural history]*

if a lion calls and you walk not just to but into
a bear park for real   say something about a wedding then think
that was the june wedding   two years ago
time pulse   this rum is new   it's not bad
thought no way she'd remember me but hell first thing
he was here yesterday
and i thought good to know a bear still running
kerosene and fumes   if when
a lion calls you have rum then
walk into a bear park   that's all that's it
to know what i'm doing and where else i've been
there is no guarantee
and if i make this deal or that we can only hope i keep it
jacarandas   if a bear were there
for sure sitting at the bar or on the chair next and if not then   later
he would have shown me his teeth
and i would have plunged   fully   into
remember i wanted no less for myself
just i displace things as though
in a bath except   today was my birthday   classic
one would say to be kind
and this much is true i never drank rum with you
although who knows of course we may have
considering   so let's say this much is true probably
i never drank rum with you
and my terracotta wish   for a moment feels like
enlightenment
                    ron bacardi superior
                    fabricado por bacardi y cia SA de CV
sweating little
green bottle
                    40% alc vol   *casa fondada en cuba*
the small of its back to grip
and how i gripped you there too   but know this
it's more than a little   minty
1862   just a taste i said is not for the noticing
                    i write about lovers and bottles
unscrewing their caps   to hear that gentle scraping
metal on glass relief   cleaning wound relief   that kind
                                        of

jangle in the grooves
bangle spiral   i write about lovers and bottles and if
a lion calls and i walk into a bear park and if
a bear was there yesterday and a june wedding
was two years ago what
things could be different but they're not
that's lion logic i prefer   to look to where a bear sat
through the lens of a green sheep   *superior or inferior* really
who cares i mean remember
molar fleece i mean despite i mean to spite
                facundo bacardi
sunlight and lime
there was none but it was there   anyway
rum and the lack of the historical and mint
shirt mint sheet mint juleps what
how did things get spriggish
the carving front   small of the back   shoulders
mouth lips   lover bottle
vitrine i call it a fish tank with a reminder of levels
away from the living in that way
arched back upturned head
               you are here and we are electric   just so

* After the series by Damien Hirst.

[concrete]

man with the painting mismaloya arches
in the water horseshoe cupcakes
regretfully   *they're not realistic*
and fishing pole palms bending the kind
we don't have here
and brick like cobblestones the kind
we don't have here
late birthday present dreamland
with creatures in pairs not lonely pairs
walk to his house talk of chandeliers
ostrich curiosity   crane a neck to look ostrich
laughing candles and almost like strutting
ballet dancer ostrich with pointed toes
                        climbing the ladder
flat palm warm concrete   hand chest pulse
and as to how to construct
an ostrich kitchen   half inside and half out of course
concrete beams rebar
buckets hardhat and what
                        orange pipe
the kind an ostrich needs for breathing remember
i wondered if this was the start of something i would see the finish of
ostrich on a roof
imagine it   moonlight and watering
what's concrete   an outside drying faster than an inside
                        what we call cracking

[hurricane sunset]

hurricane coming so they say so
do i have to ask what
is a lion doing in town same day
re minder lady he only wants you when in reverse
and things will not   be different this time
and true if he were here he would not be enough
my need for him or any kind of
warm cement and re the
                    re divider lady not long ago she was here with gravitas
being rather than skittering over   moving ground moving sky and
bounced off the mountain
along with peach champagne
the woman shading her eyes
hurricane coming   so they say so
do i have to ask what is a lion doing
in town same day that tunnel of water
will break an orchid leaf soon   there is only so much bending
who is to hear or understand
newspapers on the bed check dictionary
                    derrumbar
means to knock down but easy
to confuse large pans with half a gate at three in the morning
                    and there was orange pipe too

iii

boca de tomates

[crocodiles]

he said let's go to the mouth of the tomatoes
that's not south to the mouth but
the one near mile long bridge
there are crocodiles there and signs
do not get out of your car you will get eaten by crocodiles
                    historical lady
twenty four hours i knew him and thought
barefoot next to the crocodiles
not the craziest thing i'd seen
but remember *who are you who cares let's go*   circles
like baking next to the can of valvoline   i took a picture
a good one except for the branch in the mouth i will edit
that out i said but he said the branch is perfect
                    is a crocodile being a crocodile
behind and in front   in spirals
i would like to   see the next if
to see the next from this were a talent i had   to see us
                 in the street arguing or him with the what
are you taking pictures of now
hanging out of the cherry red   *get back in*
circles of branches and crocodiles and crocodiles circling
trailing crocodile swish
under ficus and mangrove mixmaster crocodile
for real   all it took   *suck it up*
come wish me happy birthday
chip birthday
and he did not even have cake
but we had tacos come here come closer there's always
tacos but this time he had quesadillas

[blue flames]

and i thought how did i know
cowboy hat and sunglasses that you   would never take them off
again   next to a sea lion and to hook my arm around a sea lion
sea lion comfortable and you see how i need
some big man guru   you told a joke
a muskrat laughed a crane teetered and i
wished i wasn't there
you see this problem   personalities
it was time to throw out the postcards but i didn't
                    it's not about the people it's the poppets
on this one   thailand
thailand is not just a place i've never been
and a nation of other women but also
gemstones and thailand is
if you say you have emotions beyond the *baby this baby that*
if you say you have layers beyond the teflon cool
you say *i hate everything and everyone*
                    except you and i
am first in line
registering to believe you
                    the hurricane was a tropical storm actually and after all
how is it i'm disappointed   wanted you to run after me one time
baby this baby that
even an ostrich you can call *baby*   ostrich surprise
the way you stretched out
pagan shimmer blue flames   and that familiar spill forth
this is also you is not you is you isn't like i
still had those photographs   sayulita mist and you
emerging from some other   salt water layer
no to that and all related   lion   bear
i make up these animals
                    thinking they will protect
and even an ostrich to take me under
his big wing and no sharp teeth   seriously
who is that impervious that unkind
i said but probably not psychopathic
i make them into these animals
                    while wondering about the daughter the property manager the ex wife
what kind of flooding
i never found out about your trip   and know nothing more about mint

to go cold turkey on a lion
is never again to see a turtle house
unless you move which you might
unless you die which you might
then i will go there i will be one of those
lurking peering people   to see in from out this time

                    people look lonely when you know them even lions
lion at his most dangerous vulnerable lion
between paw pads or tender lion neck fur tender lion belly
undertow
another choice   *would be a development*
just not the right   *exactly but ah*
remember tourist season's coming   wild horse said

[green]

                if you go to a lion chip birthday next day wake up with a lion
just so   know that the start of the matter was his cool
thirty years you can't buy it can't steal it
i heard that then watched as he zoomed around
lion explaining about the bumper
                if i break it i can fix it
and i said if you didn't break it wouldn't have to
and he said where's the shrapnel in that
the woman in green was there but didn't take her serious
lion pounce over to me anyway
and those emails he wrote didn't send   i believe it or not
either way good lion talk
got me heading to where he was
we talked about the man who went missing
the other one   and there was no picking apart

                if you go to a lion chip birthday two days later move in with a lion
           and two years previous was with the other crocodiles
concentric thematic
           to go to the mouth of the tomatoes turn right
near that strip mall that stands out like
teeth against the dust and diesel
past the hugging tree and the shanties
garbage bags and blue tarp   imagine it
in rainy season i said   driftwood bramble hairball
tinderbox with thorns   candy wrapped fish head sludge
feathered carcass bottle vial oh baby
         he goes for a swim
impossible to imagine
wading the sand flat mud flat   crocodiles
can't bite when swimming he says
         need to have their feet on the ground
who told him that some random person
way out wading lion does he think crocodile immunity lion
past the crab pots and in shark trunks
when he looks back   the shore to my right

         the matter of the matter was green
with white waves between moss on driftwood he said
take a picture of this   valley with

breathing holes whale back green
and holding out his hand for me but i said this green
will not come out against the sun this color
will not appear as we see it in front of our eyes
                    he said but give it a try and i said ok and we did

[teak]

chronological how about   the drive to his house
steam on the dash smoke on the hood
water into the tank hot bubbling
was that rock to blame the one you said there is big rock
            middle of the road and i said
should have been more clear maybe
instructional directive   i had just turned looked back
strained mattress black walls
half full *garrafón* empty   clothes rack
alleyway and three dogs
          where is my plan b
lion says i should have one not for nothing
tell him i do not live life with plan b's
the fallen teak leaves are crisp as kindling and big as our bed
but he says come
          parade around town my newest victim
but i say they have seen me before they know
i am your same old victim and if you make it seem
your line of women was last week ok
hand to ground the whole town loved an opera singer
whereas i can barely hold a note
plan b's grow tall like teak
and with dapples and knots
only one at his gate and yet
          he can say one of them too high
and one of them too low

[cake]

once i said to slice through once   like strawberry
cheesecake or cinnamon to slice through
once
to say what you think and mean
you said what then   and what would be the point of that
       empathy was a dead bug on its back
wouldn't sit up right
and a hornet's nest that was compassion   our counterfellows
       while the cinnamon crumbles the crust is too dry
the cheesecake is not new york cheesecake the chocolate is soggy
and the color of the graveyard the night
you dropped the *information*   time bomb
i am just temporary
boarder in a turtle house
i heard applause from far off maybe the dinosaurs maybe
       the palms and empathy i asked what is it
and how to convince you otherwise
you went for a walk
and when you came back black on black   i couldn't tell
if you were loving it or partially   is this what we call
left by the side of the road again
sure
it made me feel like back in the sort of circus
life i thought almost forgotten about
big guru lion when you came back   black on black
i said once to slice through like strawberry
       cheesecake or cinnamon
but you agreed what would be the point of that

[umberglow]

denver omelette nature's detail sense of time and already
                    i had my shoes off
soon i will have no need for shoes
they will not be one of my encumbrances like i said unencumbered
like you said on your ass like i shrugged
outside home depot on the catnip
                   duncan falls taste of summer alfalfa
garden chair   feet dangling
paint swatches   to shuffle they are rough
on the paint side and the other
smooth   *you do not have*
all the information but now i have some
still you buy the blinds
you are going to hang them   *for privacy*
          how you ape these words that are not yours
my wild man turned curbside appeal
all the calamities   the dryer the driveway the rock wall
neighborhood gossip and
shoddy workmanship oh my curtain
i've never seen so many shields barriers fences
blinds in the truck means going slow   here at last is some layered cargo
but why did you wave it in my face *the information*
         i didn't have
there are things we need but instead
hang a cigarette out the window say
crema de limón   both times
i missed it when we passed the dinosaurs although you said
when we passed the crane   end of the line crane
denver omelette nature's detail sense of time and already
         we talk of *riesgo neutro*
and umberglow that's *brillo ocre oscuro*

[pool]

i

polynesian village in mexico i can't get it how
pretty soon the hills will be filled
something done but not finished
everyone builds here no one wants to stay
        these mushroom houses are dying
to be bought you can see it in their tiki
tacky trying to be superficial enough
what i tried for too   circus days
if we go on a fact finding mission we will find this town is all frontdrop
behind it's disneyland or a movie set
little mosquito swamp
choking on golf carts yoga panted ticky
lobster taco duck coffee
        if it wasn't for ddt
none of this would have happened

ii

if you think a rock wall can become so important how about a pool
is like a baby with all the products
and medications for this and that
        plastic windows color
coded boric acid
a devourer   it's taken all the showering water
and leave it alone one day   it's green
fluorescent   imagine it
and did you know the surf is right there
a pool is a big bath fundamentally
who needs it   fundamentally
at the side there is a room
some sort of m machine   some sort of moloch
        the things we were where did they go
a lion with a pool   does not go to the beach anymore

iii

if you're not going forwards you're going back
he says but i say can't we stand still

                    now the mega it was not such a big deal
except in the way it hurt my eyes my feet my heart
i did not want to go in there
or come out loaded with more
than they have in their houses
the houses we zoom past with people in front
torn curtains and sackcloth and holes in the walls
and they are out   talking laughing while we
grim faced transport
                    what is this stuff and why is it needed
back to the private driveway
up the private staircase
                    into this vast privacy
we are people   carrying
more than i had in my whole little life house
that's not an exaggeration
up and down   that's not an exaggeration
i couldn't even   imagine it
how did i end up here
fine in my cave with centipedes on the floor
leaking roof and single bag of groceries
am going to stop calling that life little it was
                    unencumbered
swimming pool big screen tv mega
you call it an upgrade i say i will trade you
back to how it was
                    and how we were   imagine it
pause near the garbage turn mist
cobblestones don't step on a toad

[small island island]

in la peñita under the sea horses i say that's isla islote
small island island   *and why do you look so happy*
is it because it doesn't matter anymore
what's it but we'll never know   just that it's empty
next to a doorway missing a wall palm shadows
in the sand like fish skeletons or
in rincón de guayabitos   *and why do you look so happy*
i say because i did not want to know that man anyway
i am merely the day tripping object of your contempt and
                    i need you to tell me how
that hotel they call it a decamaron
with rolling lawn like the algae lake in lo de marcos
                    and how before i did not notice
                    in san pancho   it's too risky
but in chacala next to the cannon
i say i am documenting this trip
you say you always do   but i have to sneak
these photographs of you   you have never liked one of them

[intersection]

pto i said please turn over
vallarta you said   compostela i said
i've never been there and b de banderas would if i could although i said
i would be like a *perrito de callejón no de playa*
under a shady tree
until the rain came   guadalajara i was there
a few times and tepic   *güero*   is what you are
empaque resellable applies to the stall
and what they are selling   ceviche
although half the word is missing actually
resell-   we make assumptions cast aspersions
two red lights and we say things that can't be unsaid
        he says i have the tongue and it's true before i stopped speaking
i called him a bug or asked if he was one   and re empathy
it's dead and not gonna get undead   flat on its dead bug back
with velvety undercarriage and is like a carriage or something for pulling
at that time there was just the three of us
compassion came later and a hornet's nest is anyway in most cases
        an afterthought and re my tree he says i will not want it
after i see his tree and i say i will always want my tree
and he says my tree is not even a bodhi tree like his tree
and i say it's my bodhi and he says what kind of bird
is my bird i will not want it after i see
        sweeping blue jay or green flame *guacamayo*
through the jungle pass   no matter
i say i will always want it   it was the original
        first time i noticed you earlier than you think
i saw not the monkey on your foot but the other   flip flop and you
on about a boat
for real i did not take you serious seeing how smooth you were with the *baby*
this *baby* that   to catch you in the flash
the perfect picture of you contains
        cheekbone shimmer
starburst on your sunglasses   *if i have two pillows i don't need you*

[eggshells]

like watching his face for when will the crack
occur like the difference between acceptance
and resignation   *congratulations*
expose yourself to annihilation
or how you said
lady here is your role   *a distractor*
and did you think you would grow up to be that
con todo
                    i thought well my hopes
                    i'm sure they're not right
and my dreams
                    i'm sure they're not right
you know back in circus days
kind of thing some of them liked to say too
columbina inca i do
feel you calling to me   sierra madres
and re divider i see your shimmering
blue   so many eggshells
                    over the floor
even in the bedroom
there is no floor left
lion if i ask you where are the eggs
it's well known *tejones* like eggs and will manifest
confabulate you could say or
                    what's a lion like to be lionized

[pufferfish]

full throttle porcupine neurotoxin and you
can cause dizziness and vomiting
numbness prickling rapid heart rate
paralysis and asphyxiation you said
          i have not broken you   *yet*
your cruelty is scaleless instead you have spines
yet   you will never see me cry
you seemed disappointed to learn that
i seemed disappointed to grasp your objective
        when we are looking at each other who

are we looking at   pufferfish on the red eye with hangover
raging i say your problem not booze or a needle
        have a drink have a shot here's to us
and the time i've spent looking for   and made up excuses
no one can pursue an illusion like i can pufferfish determination
your poison is   misfelt silk
your spines are plastic spoons to ladle it on
your *i'm mean baby and i'm just fine with that*
is mostly provocation your
i hate everything and everybody has an   *except you*
        daddy i will make you love me
pufferfish into the maw with bared teeth pufferfish campaign
if you eat me i will turn pincushion and then you will be more than
sorry   kamikaze pufferfish
daddy i will make you notice me
like the driftwood i picked up
the coconut husk and shell
how you put them to the side along with empathy
and compassion
i believed i saw your heart
although we had eaten all the marshmallows

i believed i saw your heart
under the pagan shimmer
with oval eyes at an angle just so
wonky headlights   shifty
pufferfish in cheap suit at the bus stop with briefcase
in the rain pufferfish inflatable but otherwise won't budge
boxy pufferfish   reminds me of not you in your *baby this*

baby that but with rare shuffle trip pufferfish stammer
trying to impress of course we are not one thing
a defense mechanism to
turn yourself into something unpalatable
with stripes and spots   you never asked me
if those go together but how i loved your embarrassing
wardrobe and pufferfish   pillow if it wasn't for your spines
if i have to explain to you
what is empathy anyway
and dumb it down pufferfish   i believed i saw your heart
                                               i believed i saw my heart

iv

carricitos

[carricitos]

pick a starting point and it can't be
when I saw your lion shoulder or
when you dipped your sunglasses said
if i break it i can fix it and what
we're like when after we can say we must have been
dreaming   carricitos
last day i said yes
                    there is a greyhouse behind the branches and boulders
grey pillars and missing walls   where i dropped my flip flops
because you did and you said they will be fine
and if they are not *i will buy you new flip flops*   you and your
vast carelessness   on the rocks
take my hand and i did
but with the other going for ground
hand to ground   *things could be different but they're not*
carricitos when we are looking out over we are looking
back
                    the palm the huanacaxtle the blue jays' tails
six years ago you were here   recurring
to hide in plain sight this beach   knows it
although this is not the real secret
the real secret is something inside that thing the color of
a coconut when there is a brown and a yellow and a green
in front of a log with paw prints   seriously
looked like a big cat and those rocks were like paws
treacle between the pads
imagine it   what is the image i will hold of you now
where is that photograph
postdated you said supervening i said following
your blue flames
people drown here
when the thing to do is let it take you
people fight and they drown
                    in the spare room with curtains drawn
that i can
pack up my life in twenty minutes you called it
astonishing i called it   dawdling
box with edges like fence posts or rebar   this representation of
reinforcement on a box
i say there is no point

staying if just to tomorrow   i want to leave with this photograph
what we're like when after we can say we were dreaming
                    this happened too
there are so many paths everywhere
i cannot proceed in order
                    day of the dead we crossed the stream
aguar los duendes as you held out your hand
like to a child *hup*   i *hupped* and was on the other side
arm against your side where you were
                    soft belly lion
the graveyard was burning white crosses and hearts

up close to see the jagged cuts in the canvas
and how the back was attached with staples
                    wearing your chiang mai muay thai pad thai
you bought chocolate cake and please
tell me the things that are not *in it* i didn't say
                    please tell me all the things it is   *not*
two spoons and what
would happen if i moved mine over
would i see the flash hear the click of teeth
how many things can we say more than once
that we will then think are true
                    to cast aspersions when what i wanted to   amend
carricitos   you camped here
when a turtle house was a napkin sketch
and a model with popsicle sticks
to amend
                    everything should have been harvested then and at least
i said it's beautiful what you built
when what i meant was because it was you and yours

what happens when you finish a house
well you just have to leave it   start over
and to address it finally   your teeth
were not bear like with a need to hide them
yet you did not smile often and there are no pictures
of you smiling
                    this is not you this is not yours you are not this
but leaning over to prop up the sign *camino termina* you were
astonishing saying baby i hate you but it's a joke you were
astonishing saying that oil palm was very old you were

astonishing up the path carrying my flip flops   re minder

64

you liked to see me suffer
                    redivider lady i do
feel you calling to me
things could have been different they really could have
a path was just a path
it was nothing it was a dream it was everything abandon
given a shot of reality sounds
not like palms in the wind smells
not like burning banana
leaves in your driveway
                    cowboy hat and you
are blowing out now   into the white light burning
i could not even photograph it

what did you think of that oil palm
                    stranger

except that it was old

and did you notice the greyhouse
what about the coconuts what
was the sun on your back
and what did green look like to you

Notes

La Lancha: a surf beach near Punta Mita (in the state of) Nayarit – between Sayulita and Puerto Vallarta.

estacionamiento exclusivo: signage that appears in parking places designated for handicapped drivers.

surtidora: a department store.

elote: corn cob.

vaso: cup.

tejón: a coati/coatimundi.

huanacaxtle: parota (tree). La Cruz de Huanacaxtle is also a town, north of Puerto Vallarta, in Nayarit.

pastor: pork.

cabeza: head. E.g., *tacos de cabeza.*

surtidos: assorted, mixed (meat).

carnitas: mixed meat also, usually pork.

garrafones: large containers holding twenty liters (of drinking water).

Mega: a large chain store, like a Wal-Mart or a Target.

chicle: chewing gum.

higuera: fig tree. Higuera Blanca ("White Fig Tree") is also a town, north of Puerto Vallarta, in Nayarit.

Insurgentes: one of the main streets in downtown Puerto Vallarta.

Kukulkán: another name for Quetzalcoatl, the plumed serpent. Also the El Castillo pyramid at Chichén Itzá.

cabeza, *labio* and *lengua*: head, lips, and tongue.

callejon: alleyway.

jabón neutro: neutral soap.

jacarandas: jacarandas, also Jacarandas – a street in downtown Puerto Vallarta.

talavera: a type of tile.

Boca de Tomates: ("Mouth of the Tomatoes") an area just north of Puerto Vallarta, known for its crocodiles.

brillo ocre oscuro: brilliant dark ochre.

Sayulita: a town and popular tourist spot north of Puerto Vallarta, where the lion lives.

DDT: "Sayulita" means "little mosquito swamp." The area was uninhabitable until they invented DDT.

güero (a): a blonde and/or a light-skinned person in Mexico.

Playa Carricitos: Carricitos Beach, near Sayulita. Sometimes spelt "Carrizitos;" possibly meaning "little reeds."

aguar los duendes: literally, "to throw water on the spirits;" guard against the spirits.

camino termina: dead end.

Acknowledgements

These poems have appeared previously in the following fine publications:

"[path]" in *Commas and Colons*.
"[taxi] in *Dinosaur Bees*.
"[eye]" in *Toe Good*.
"[turtle herding]" & "[mega]" in *Press 1*.
"[teeth]" in *Stoked*.
"[ostrich] in *Her Royal Majesty*.
"[the lion and the ostrich]" in *The Conium Review*.
"[carricitos]" in the *BluePrintReview*.

About the Author

Rose Hunter's book of poetry, *to the river*, was published in 2010 by Artistically Declined Press. She published *A Foal Poem* in 2011, and *You As Poems* in 2012. She is from Australia originally, lived in Canada for many years, and now lives in Puerto Vallarta, Mexico. Links to more of her writing can be found at "Whoever Brought Me Here Will Have To Take Me Home" (roseh400.wordpress.com).

www.ingramcontent.com/pod-product-compliance
Lightning Source LLC
LaVergne TN
LVHW061229060426
835509LV00012B/1473